Lavished in Love

Daily Short Lenten Meditations

Dr. Marcus B. Peter

Credo Publishing

an imprint of

En Route Books and Media, LLC
Saint Louis, MO

Credo Publishing, an imprint of En Route Books and Media, LLC

5705 Rhodes Avenue

St. Louis, MO 63109

Contact us at
contactus@enroutebooksandmedia.com

Cover Credit: Marcus Peter

Copyright 2026 Marcus Peter

ISBN-13: 979-8-88870-499-8

Library of Congress Control Number: 2026933270

Scripture passages have been taken from the Revised Standard Version, Catholic Edition of the Bible. Copyright 1971 by the Division of Christian Education of the National Council of the Churches of Christ in the USA.

Excerpts from the English translation of the *Catechism of the Catholic Church* for the United States of America. Copyright 1994, United States Catholic Conference, Inc. - Libreria Editrice Vaticana.

All rights reserved. No part of this book may be reproduced, stored in a retrieval system, or transmitted in any form, or by any means, electronic, mechanical, photocopying, or otherwise, without the prior written permission of the author.

For the listeners and patrons of Ave Maria Radio and the Kresta Institute.

May this book bring about a deeper transformation in your life of holiness.

Table of Contents

Foreword v

Introduction 1

Ash Wednesday 3

    Thursday After Ash Wednesday 5

    Friday after Ash Wednesday 7

    Saturday after Ash Wednesday 9

First Sunday of Lent 11

    Monday of Week One 13

    Tuesday of Week One 15

    Wednesday of Week One 17

    Thursday of Week One 19

    Friday of Week One 21

    Saturday of Week One 23

Second Sunday of Lent 25

    Monday of Week Two 27

    Tuesday of Week Two 29

    Wednesday of Week Two 31

    Thursday of Week Two 33

Friday of Week Two 35

Saturday of Week Two 37

Third Sunday of Lent 39

Monday of Week Three 41

Tuesday of Week Three 43

Wednesday of Week Three 45

Thursday of Week Three 47

Friday of Week Three 49

Saturday of Week Three 51

Fourth Sunday of Lent 53

Monday of Week Four 55

Tuesday of Week Four 57

Wednesday of Week Four 59

Thursday of Week Four 61

Friday of Week Four 63

Saturday of Week Four 65

Fifth Sunday of Lent 67

Monday of Week Five 69

Tuesday of Week Five 71

Wednesday of Week Five 73

Table of Contents

- Thursday of Week Five ... 75
- Friday of Week Five ... 77
- Saturday of Week Five ... 79
- Palm Sunday ... 81
  - Monday of Holy Week ... 83
  - Tuesday of Holy Week ... 85
  - Wednesday of Holy Week ... 87
  - Holy Thursday ... 89
  - Good Friday ... 91
  - Holy Saturday ... 93
- Easter Sunday ... 95
- Conclusion ... 97

Foreword

Christian life is not lived in abstraction. We are physical beings, bound by space and time. The Church, in her wisdom, has given us patterns of time through which we can recognize the rhythms of God's incarnational grace. This grace takes form in history and helps shape our bodies, our calendars, and our souls to the life of Christ.

In a world ruled by fiscal quarters and academic semesters, it is a gift to be reminded that there is another calendar. One that integrates our lives into the story of God and His work in creation. The liturgical year is a slow catechesis in love. It is a sacred syllabus that forms us in the mystery of Christ. Like a screw, its annual cycles dig the mystery of Christ's life, death, resurrection, and continued reign more deeply into our lives.

The Incarnation did not happen in a vacuum. It occurred in a particular season, in a particular place, and involved a particular body. As an incarnational people with an incarnational faith, we must allow our own particularity to reorder our lives. The world we inhabit is a kind of fifth Gospel, declaring—as the psalmist says in Psalm 19—the very glory of God.

As we navigate this world, created good by God, and live in the time He has placed us in, we must view each season as a waystation on the pilgrimage toward heaven. The liturgical year becomes a compass for our soul. It points us toward Christ and reminds us that our destination is heaven. It allows us not only to remember the life of Christ but to inhabit it. We make the Incarnation a place in which we live and through which we are fed with the bread of heaven.

The liturgical rhythm reminds us of the story we are living so that we do not begin to pursue a narrative where we become the protagonist. We are always called to recognize the good God who has been working from the beginning to accomplish the ends He has faithfully promised to bring to consummation. Through this story, we learn that there is a victor, and His name is Jesus Christ.

To celebrate Lent is to be slowly stitched more deeply into the Passion of Christ. Every sacrifice we make, every prayer, every act of generosity becomes a thread of mercy that connects us to His suffering, His resurrection, and ultimately to the hope we have in the Paschal culmination of Easter.

Lent helps us remember the path of baptism through which we were brought into the Church. It reminds us—bodily and spiritually—of the dying we did with Christ in hope of rising with Him. In a world full of loud and bright distractions, Lent invites us to dim the lights and recognize the flame of faith Christ has ignited in our hearts. Through His mercy, our asceticism in this season adds fuel to that flame so that we might become a blazing fire of God's love in a world that, despite its noise and access, remains truly poor and lost in darkness.

Lent offers us a mirror to recognize the work of Christ in our lives, our need for redemption, and our participation in the brokenness that Christ came to redeem. It is a season to develop practices that form the posture of the penitent. We kneel before the mystery of God and bow, humbled by His extravagant grace and the means by which He has won our salvation. We follow the example of Christ in being emptied, with the hope that in Him we may be raised up.

The following pages are meant to help you walk through this season with my dear friend Marcus Peter. His reflections are honest, prayerful, and powerfully incarnational. This book is not a manual on how to live the Christian life. It is a companion along the journey. Each day, Marcus offers a doorway into deeper communion and helps us recognize the mystery that surrounds us.

Marcus is a man who, from personal experience, brings his whole heart into his love of God, his love of Scripture, and his reverence for the tradition of the Church. I am grateful that he is willing to share the fruits of his life and study to help us live more faithfully in the rhythms of this powerful season.

I pray that each day you return to these reflections and find your own questions echoed. May you hear the resonance of the Church's wisdom and the Scriptures in the pages that follow. May this Lenten season be one of great grace in your life, and may we arrive together, transformed, to celebrate our risen Lord.

May God guide you each day this season by His grace. May the grace of our Lord Jesus Christ, and the love of God, and the communion of the Holy Spirit be with you all this Lent. **AMEN**

Dr. Billy Kangas,
on the Memorial of Pope St Callistus I
2025

Introduction

Lent is upon us again. With each passing year, it is easy to develop a sense of familiarity and even nonchalance with the different seasons that make up the rhythm of the liturgical life of the Church. Yet, I'd like to put to you that Holy Mother Church uses these different seasons in the liturgical year to rouse us from spiritual slumber. It's all too easy for us to want to "fall asleep" as it were, in our spiritual life. The Church, being the good mother that she is, gives us a gentle awakening, reminding us that there is a need for us to wake up and pay attention. In the Lenten season, she wants us to be reminded of the fact that we will die.

That may sound morbid, and yet nothing could be truer. We will one day face mortal death. And when we do, we, all of us, will stand before the Lord our God, Jesus Christ, and face judgment for our thoughts, words, and actions. In the Catechism of the Catholic Church, the Magisterium reminds us that "Each man receives his eternal retribution in his immortal soul at the very moment of his death, in a particular judgment that refers his life to Christ: either entrance into the blessedness of heaven-through a purification, or immediately, or immediate and everlasting damnation" (CCC 1022). The Church has repeated, throughout the ages,

Christ's call for us to "repent and believe in the Gospel" (cf. Mark 1:15).

In this booklet and in our Lenten Mission, I would like to invite you and I to do just that. This booklet will serve as a companion to the preached Lenten Mission that you will find on each Lenten episode of *Unveiling the Covenants* (video or audio). The episodes will present to you the readings and the symbols and the imagery of each key point in the Lenten season. This booklet will allow you and your family to pray through and immerse yourself daily into each day of lent. Each day's readings will contain one quote, a small meditation, and a prayer. The objective is to keep this simple and enjoyable. Yes, enjoyable. There is a sweetness to Lent. The deeper we savor it, the sweeter it becomes for us.

The Christian who lives life in Christ need not ever fear death because he has died a thousand times over before. In Lent, the Church calls us to die to ourselves. The more willingly we embrace this call to die to ourselves, the happier we will inevitably be, because we will be that much freer to embrace the love of Jesus Christ. This is my hope for you. May this Lenten season be your most transformative one yet.

Ash Wednesday

"The Lenten season offers us once again an opportunity to reflect upon the very heart of Christian life: charity. This is a favorable time to renew our journey of faith, both as individuals and as a community, with the help of the word of God and the sacraments. This journey is one marked by prayer and sharing, silence and fasting, in anticipation of the joy of Easter."

- Pope Benedict XVI, Lenten Message, 2012

Meditation:

Lent begins with Ash Wednesday because the Israelites and early Christians saw ashes as a tangible sign of death. *Memento Mori,* the Latin Church calls it. The "memory of death." When we don the ashes upon ourselves, we are wearing the sign of our mortality. We proclaim to the world, "I recognize that I will die one day. I wish to strive to live like that." This week, I'd like to invite you and your family to consider the ways in which we are not yet ready to meet our Lord. Lent is a time of surrender. Let us trust that He is the Lord of our life.

Prayer:

Lord, grant me the grace to receive more of your life into my own. Grant me the grace to detach from disordered desires and to hold on to you. Grant me and my family the grace of a joyous Lenten season. Amen.

Thursday After Ash Wednesday

"Each year, the Lenten Season is set before us as a good opportunity for the intensification of prayer and penance, opening hearts to the docile welcoming of the divine will. During Lent, a spiritual journey is outlined for us that prepares\ us to relive the Great Mystery of the Death and Resurrection of Christ. This is done primarily by listening to the Word of God more devoutly and by practicing mortification more generously, thanks to which it is possible to render greater assistance to those in need."

- Pope St. John Paul II, Lenten Message, 2005

Meditation:

Lent is a time to be concerned for our spiritual life. It is a time for us to do soul searching and an examination of our conscience. It is a time to let the Lord set right what is within us. From there, the season of Lent then compels us to be concerned for each other, to stir a response within us in love and good works for the good of our neighbor. Christ has won us forgiveness. He is our High Priest who has sacrificed His life for us. Embracing that forgiveness means also acknowledging how we have sinned and wronged others.

Prayer:

Lord, I know that I need to keep praying to sustain my life in you. Grant me the grace to deepen my prayer life with you. Illuminate my life that I may be honest about my own failings, and to confess them sincerely. Plant in me a desire to be ever more reconciled to you each day. Amen.

Friday after Ash Wednesday

"Even now, says the LORD, return to me with your whole heart, with fasting, and weeping, and mourning; Rend your hearts, not your garments, and return to the LORD, your God."

- Joel 2: 12-13

Meditation:

Jesus Christ, Our Lord, Himself blessed and hallowed the 40 day fast that we are in when He put Himself through such an experience in the wilderness. He doesn't demand of us what He Himself was not willing to do in far greater intensity. He is calling us to be very honest with the depths of our hearts. What lies there? What is within us? What do we hide from Him or from the world? Our Lenten acts of fasting, prayer, almsgiving, and penance are meant to open our souls to the light of God's grace. Be unafraid to let Him take those things within us that stop us from giving our whole selves to Him.

Prayer:

Lord, I am aware of my deep need for you, and yet I am still not as aware of it as I should be. Deepen my awareness of how much I need you. Heal me of the parts of my inner life that I hold on to or hide. Take them. Be the Lord of my heart, and transform me into the son/daughter you want me to be. Amen.

Saturday after Ash Wednesday

A clean heart create for me, O God,
and a steadfast spirit renew within me.
Cast me not out from your presence,
and your Holy Spirit take not from me.
Give me back the joy of your salvation,
and a willing spirit sustain in me.
O Lord, open my lips
and my mouth shall proclaim your praise.

- Psalm 51: 14; 17

Meditation:

The heart is the deepest part of us, according to the Church's teaching. It isn't about our emotions, as many of us would think. Instead, it reflects the deepest, truest part of our beings. For St. Augustine, the heart is where God is already present to us, even if the person isn't aware of it yet. Lent is a time when God wants to do a deep cleansing of our hearts, as David is writing about in the Psalm above. Our sins may injure or cut off the life of grace within us, but God relentlessly reaches out to us for the sole purpose of saving us and drawing us back to Him. He wants to do this for you every day of your life, especially this Lenten season.

Prayer:

Lord, I know of the state of my heart and yet even I must admit that I am blind to so much that is within it. Please come into my heart. Come flood me with your grace. Come fill me with your life. Heal my heart of sin and its attachments. I want to see myself as you see me. Let me be entirely yours. Amen.

First Sunday of Lent

"When I bring clouds over the earth, and the bow appears in the clouds, I will recall the covenant I have made between me and you and all living beings, so that the waters shall never again become a flood to destroy all mortal beings."

- Gen 9:15

Meditation:

It can be difficult for us to understand a loving God who would perform an act of justice like the flood. Yet, in God, love and justice are not separate, they are one and the same. We often make the mistake of thinking that mercy and love negate justice when the opposite is true. When God shows mercy, He perfects justice and He is Love. He calls us to do the same. We cannot expect true forgiveness if we are not sorry for the sins that we have committed. The Church calls us to understand that sorrow for sins means, firstly, a willingness to acknowledge my sin, secondly, a repentance of the action I have done, and thirdly, a firm purpose of amendment. The Christian life calls us to ever grow in virtue. While God doesn't expect immediate perfection of us on this earth, He does, in fact, want to make us perfect as He is perfect 9cf. Matt 5:8).

Prayer:

Lord, by the waters of Baptism, you cleansed my soul from sin and welcomed me into your covenant family. Renew the grace of my baptism and convert me more and more. Grant me true sorrow for my sins and set me free of all of them. Amen.

Monday of Week One

"The waters of the great flood you made a sign of the waters of Baptism, that make an end of sin and a new beginning of goodness.

- Roman Missal, Easter Vigil 42: Blessing of Water

Meditation:

Our baptism united us to the death of Christ. That is why it is a sacrament of new life. The Church has always taught that in baptism, we die with Christ. Baptism joins us to Jesus's sacrifice on the Cross. Not just at the moment of our baptism, but, from that point on, for the rest of our lives. This is an unthinkable mystery and yet it is what we receive as a heritage as children of God. It is because we are joined to Jesus's sacrifice that we can receive the benefit of the price being paid for our sins. Christ paid a debt He didn't owe because we owed a debt we couldn't pay.

Prayer:

Lord, today, I pray for the grace to be ever more faithful to my baptism. I am marked as your child. I carry upon my soul the seal of being a member of your family. This is a gift I do not want to take for granted. Help me live in a manner that is worthy of being called a baptized child of my Father in Heaven. Amen.

Tuesday of Week One

"Baptism, which corresponds to this, now saves you, not as a removal of dirt from the body but as an appeal to God for a clear conscience, through the resurrection of Jesus Christ, who has gone into heaven and is at the right hand of God, with angels, authorities, and powers subject to him."

- 1 Peter 3:21-22

Meditation:

Our baptism has made us new creatures. Every day that we live in sanctifying grace, every time we make the sign of the Cross with holy water, we renew our baptismal sacrament. We are granted new mercy and grace every single day, especially when we attend the liturgy of the Mass. We receive, at Mass, the forgiveness of all our venial sins. In the Sacrament of Reconciliation, we receive the forgiveness of all our mortal sins. God's Fatherly love is unending and He provides so many means for us to come back into His life of grace because He knows that that is the only path to our happiness.

Prayer:

Lord, I know your plan is for my happiness. Help me see that that happiness means possessing you in my life as my perfect good. Everything else should be secondary. Please reorder my life so that you are my first and truest love. Amen.

Wednesday of Week One

"Holy Baptism is the basis of the whole Christian life, the gateway to life in the Spirit and the door which gives access to the other sacraments. Through Baptism we are freed from sin and reborn as sons of God; we become members of Christ, are incorporated into the Church and made sharers in her mission: 'Baptism is the sacrament of regeneration through water in the word.'"

- CCC 1213

Meditation:

Salvation is a free gift but it comes with a price, and that price is the entirety of our lives. It isn't sufficient that our faith in Christ be a part of our lives. Christ calls for us to love Him above everyone and everything else in our lives. He calls us to realize that, like Paul, we are to have Him as our "all in all," (cf. 1 Cor 15:28). When we make for ourselves idols of people, relationships, or things; when we make these things greater than God in our life, we find ourselves progressively sadder, unfulfilled, and miserable. They become the chains that bind us. We become slaves to them. And Jesus wants to set us free from that. The only way to that freedom is through Him.

Prayer:

Lord, please set me free from the chains that bind me. I am unhappy when I have anything else in my life that is greater than you. I want you to be my Lord, my God, my savior, my healer, my friend, and my first Love. Amen.

Thursday of Week One

"After John had been arrested, Jesus came to Galilee proclaiming the gospel of God: 'This is the time of fulfillment. The kingdom of God is at hand. Repent, and believe in the gospel.'"

- Mk 1:12-15

Meditation:

The Son of God becoming Man was a definitive moment in human history. His birth, life, ministry, passion, death, resurrection, and ascension are all historically undeniable facts. This prompts you and I to have to honestly answer Christ's question ourselves, "who do you say that I am?" (cf. Matt 16:15). If Jesus Christ is truly God who became man, that should change everything about the way I live. If I profess faith in Him, that should captivate my entire being. If eternal life is what He says it is, then the only thing that matters in this life is living so as to enter into the joy of God with the saints in Heaven.

Prayer:

I cannot possibly live out your call for my life by my own strength, so I thank you from the depths of my heart for your sanctifying and sacramental graces that allow me to daily be more and more conformed into your image. I want to be like you. I want to live for you. Please be Lord over my entire life. Amen.

Friday of Week One

*"Your ways, O Lord, are love and truth to those who keep
your covenant.
Remember that your compassion, O LORD,
and your love are from of old.
In your kindness remember me,
because of your goodness, O LORD."*

- Psalm 25:6-7

Meditation:

Loving Jesus and professing faith in Him means living out what it means to be a follower of Jesus in all facets of our life. It is all too easy to think that being a Christian means being a nice person. That's the furthest thing from the truth. A Christian is one who strives to keep all of the commandments of Christ and His Church. A Christian is one who knows that life in Christ means a life conformed to His teachings and how He wants us to live. A Christian recognizes that this isn't easy, especially when it comes to morality, and yet, the Christian chooses to follow Christ. Not only when we understand His teachings but, I argue, especially when we don't. Our profession of faith means assenting our minds and lives to Jesus entirely, trusting Him to teach and guide us into all truth every day for our entire lives.

Prayer:

Lord, I sometimes don't quite understand the teachings you call me to follow, but I do know that you love me and that this is what you know is best for me. Grant me the grace to live by your teachings always. Amen.

Saturday of Week One

"If you suffer with Him, you will reign with Him. If you cry with Him, you will have joy with Him. If you die with Him on the Cross of tribulation, you will possess the eternal dwelling place in the splendor of the saints. And your name, written in the Book of Life, will be glorious among men."

- St. Clare of Assisi

Meditation:

The sufferings we endure in this world cannot begin to compare with the joys and the glory that we have awaiting us in eternal life. In our times of pain and heartache, however, it is much easier to simply be consumed by the pain and the trial. In the face of this, especially during this season of Lent, let us turn to our Lord in a sense of surrender and hope not only that God will bring us the justice we desire, but that He will bless our faithfulness to Him. Our life on this earth is not in vain. We are meriting for ourselves a deeper participation in God's own majestic glory in eternal life. This is only possible because of Jesus's sacrifice. He has made every ounce of suffering we endure on earth a sacrifice that we can offer to the Lord for our own growth in holiness and for the sake of our friends, loved ones, and the souls in purgatory.

Prayer:

Lord, take my pain and suffering. I offer them all to you as a sacrifice united to your sacrifice on the Cross. Use my sufferings for your will. Make me holier through them. Amen

Second Sunday of Lent

"By myself I have sworn, says the Lord, because you have done this, and have not withheld your son, your only son, I will indeed bless you, and I will multiply your descendants as the stars of heaven and as the sand which is on the seashore. And your descendants shall possess the gate of their enemies, and by your descendants shall all the nations of the earth bless themselves, because you have obeyed my voice."

- Gen 22:16-18

Meditation:

God's call to Abraham to bring his only son, Isaac, up Mount Moriah to be sacrificed is perhaps one of the most inscrutable parts of Scripture. Yet the core of the story isn't the act of sacrifice itself, but Abraham's faith that YHWH was going to be faithful to all the promises He had made to Abraham as part of the covenant they shared. Those promises were to be fulfilled through Isaac, which only meant that Abraham knew that YHWH was going to have Isaac live through the ordeal somehow. This was the real test for Abraham. Whether he could bring himself to trust God's promises for his life.

Prayer:

Lord, in times of trial, I want to be in control. In those times, trusting upon your promises for me is perhaps the most difficult thing I can do. Please grant me the grace to do so, especially when I am tested. Open my heart to see how good a Father you are to me. Amen

Monday of Week Two

"Let us then cling to his blessing, and let us see what are the ways of blessedness. Let us recall the events of old. Why was our father Abraham blessed? Was it not because he performed justice and truth through faith? Isaac, knowing the future in confidence, was willingly led forth as a sacrifice."

- Pope St. Clement of Rome

Meditation:

Many of the Church Fathers and Jewish Rabbis teach that Isaac was a willing participant in the entire sacrifice event. He willingly chose to climb the mountain with his father, knowing that he was the sacrificial victim. Hence, they posit that the faith that was demonstrated here wasn't just by Abraham, but also by Isaac's willingness. The faith of the father is now shown to be the faith of the child as well. In our own families, it is precisely how fully we live our own faith that invites our children to do the same. Instead of something imposed upon them, the life of faith ought to be something children are invited into in witnessing their mother and father live it out.

Prayer:

Lord, I want my faith in you to be so fully lived out that all the members of my family are invited to live it out with me as well. I know I am not a perfect witness of you, yet grant me the grace to be a good one. One that shines with the light of your own grace. Amen

Tuesday of Week Two

"You don't know how to pray? Put yourself in the presence of God, and as soon as you have said, 'Lord, I don't know how to pray!' you can be sure you've already begun."

- St. Josemaría Escrivá

Meditation:

Sometimes, it seems that people think just because a person is a Christian, they are automatically masters of prayer. The fact of the matter is prayer, like all things in our life of faith, must be a trained discipline. It does, however, start very simply. Prayer is the act of communing with God. A simple conversation with God is an act of prayer. This lent, let's strive to build the kind of relationship with God wherein we are always talking with Him through the day like we would our best friend who is beside us through the day. God doesn't need us to pray to Him. He already knows what we want and need. Yet, He wants us to pray to Him because, in doing so, we are consciously putting in His hands the things in our hearts and minds that are weighing us down. Prayer allows us to be more surrendered to God's love.

Prayer:

Lord, help me develop a deeper, more intimate prayer life with you. I want a living and active prayer life that unites me constantly to you. Amen

Wednesday of Week Two

"As a final stage in the purification of his faith, Abraham, 'who had received the promises,' is asked to sacrifice the son God had given him. Abraham's faith does not weaken ('God himself will provide the lamb for a burnt offering.'), for he 'considered that God was able to raise men even from the dead.' And so the father of believers is conformed to the likeness of the Father who will not spare his own Son but will deliver him up for us all. Prayer restores man to God's likeness and enables him to share in the power of God's love that saves the multitude."

- CCC 2572

Meditation:

God the Father loves us just the way we are, but He loves us far too deeply to let us stay that way. He knows that we are made for so much more, and rightfully so: He made us! He wants to keep converting, transforming, and purifying us every single day of our lives. He challenges us daily to break out of worldly mediocrity. He made us for Sainthood. Every one of us. He wants us to be excellent. This isn't a special call for the elect. This is the destiny of all of His children, including you and me.

Prayer:

Lord, purify me and make me a Saint. I don't know what that means, I don't understand what that entails, but I do know that this is what you made me for, so make me a Saint. Amen.

Thursday of Week Two

"We encounter patches of light, but we also encounter stretches in which God seems absent, when his silence weighs on our hearts and his will does not correspond with ours, with our inclination to do as we like. However, the more we open ourselves to God, welcome the gift of faith and put our whole trust in him — like Abraham, like Mary — the more capable he will make us, with his presence, of living every situation of life in peace and assured of his faithfulness and his love. However, this means coming out of ourselves and our own projects so that the word of God may be the lamp that guides our thoughts and actions."

- Benedict XVI, Wednesday Address, 2012

Meditation:

In times of hardship, trial, or persecution, the human temptation is to fall into ourselves, to think of our situation and our need for control over it. In those times, the easier thing to do is to seek out ways to exert control over the situation. To work out a favorable outcome for ourselves. To spare ourselves further hurt, anxiety, and heartbreak. It is tough for us to understand but in those times, our Father in Heaven desires to deliver and heal us infinitely more than we desire it ourselves.

Prayer:

Lord, help me trust you in times of trial. Help me trust that you are a good Father who is here for me. Amen.

Friday of Week Two

*"I will walk before the Lord, in the land of the living.
I believed, even when I said,
'I am greatly afflicted.'
Precious in the eyes of the LORD
is the death of his faithful ones."*

- Psalm 116:9-10

Meditation:

God is a good Father. Those words are tough to truly trust and hold on to. We experience so much pain in our life. Sufferings, relationship issues, diseases, etc. Yet, God is a good Father. He is the ultimate good Father. He wants us to cling to Him and trust Him to heal us, to deliver us, to strengthen us, to provide for us, and to protect us. He wants the greatest good for us: Eternal Heavenly Happiness with Him. He alone knows how much you and I need to be molded to be in a disposition of receiving that happiness. That's why this life in Christ is not without cost. God is calling us to absolute abandonment to His love so that He can fill us with the hope of eternal life with Him.

Prayer:

Lord, fill my mind with the goal of Heaven. Help me understand that it is only when I have my mind and heart set on Heaven that everything else in this life makes sense. Especially when it is most difficult, draw me out of myself to focus on my eternal happiness with you. Amen.

Saturday of Week Two

"Our radical belonging to Christ and the fact that 'we are in him' must imbue in us an attitude of total trust and immense joy. In short, we must indeed exclaim with St Paul: 'If God is for us, who is against us?' (Rom 8: 31). And the reply is that nothing and no one 'will be able to separate us from the love of God in Christ Jesus our Lord' (Rom 8: 39). Our Christian life, therefore, stands on the soundest and safest rock one can imagine. And from it we draw all our energy, precisely as the Apostle wrote: 'I can do all things in him who strengthens me' (Phil 4: 13)."

- Benedict XVI, Wednesday Audience, 2006

Meditation:

If we want joy, there is only one path: radical surrender to Jesus Christ. In whatever our state of life, only one path brings us joy: when our life, marriage, apostolates, finances, ambition, work, children, and all other aspects are completely given to the hands of Christ every single day. This is the only path that will give all of our life its truest meaning and purpose. When we abandon to the Lord, we don't have to shoulder the burden of everything. Christ makes our hearts light when we cast it all upon Him. He cares for us.

Prayer:

Lord, grant me the grace to cast all my burdens upon you, so that I can experience what it means to have your yoke, which is easy and light. Give me rest. Amen.

Third Sunday of Lent

"'When Love gives meaning to your life…'. Jesus brings to fulfilment the path of the Commandments with his Cross and Resurrection; he brings it to radically overcome selfishness, sin and death with the gift of himself for love. Welcoming the infinite love of God, trusting him, following the path that he has laid down, can we give deeper meaning to life and open up a future of hope."

- Pope Benedict XVI, Message, 2012

Meditation:

Everyone wants hope. We work and live in the hope of a better tomorrow than the one we have today. This drive to hope is what keeps us pursuing the good, and the true, and the beautiful. Once in a while, it is important that we ask ourselves what it is we are truly hoping for. Earthly goals have their place, but, at the end of the day, even after we attain them, they never make us completely happy or fulfilled. What we are truly longing for is a hope that will satisfy us completely. That hope has a name, and His name is Jesus. All of our work and life is driven to hope in Him, whether we realize it or not.

Prayer:

Lord, I hope for so much because, ultimately, I am hoping for you. You are my hope and my ultimate future. Help me be more aware of that so that you can order my life to reflect that hope in all I do. Amen.

Monday of Week Three

"The virtue of hope responds to the aspiration to happiness which God has placed in the heart of every man; it keeps man from discouragement; it sustains him during times of abandonment; it opens up his heart in expectation of eternal beatitude. Buoyed up by hope, he is preserved from selfishness and led to the happiness that flows from charity."

- CCC 1818

Meditation:

Hope for Heaven compels us to charity. We need to understand firstly what charity means. Charity doesn't just mean donating money to those in need, though it includes that. Charity is the highest form of love. It is selfless love or, *agape*, in the Greek. It is the love that seeks to will the good of the other over the self. Love by definition is to will the good of the other, but the Christian is called to love as charity. When we live a life of hope in Christ, charity supernaturally overflows from our life of prayer and worship. Our good works become a way in which our love of Christ becomes known and manifest. True charity must start with true love of Christ.

Prayer:

Lord, I want to be a charitable person, so fill me with the grace of loving you above all else. Help me be so filled with your love that others will experience your love in me. Amen.

Tuesday of Week Three

"Live in faith and hope, though it be in darkness, for in this darkness God protects the soul. Cast your care upon God for you are His and He will not forget you. Do not think that He is leaving you alone, for that would be to wrong Him."

- St. John of The Cross

Meditation:

Mother Teresa once noted that one of the great diseases plaguing modern society is loneliness. This is an odd sentiment considering that mankind has never been more connected to each other than today, with all our great advances in technology. Yet, what Mother Teresa was trying to point out is that, precisely because of the myriad of worldly distractions we have at our fingertips today, the thought of God and spending time with Him in prayer can sometimes be relegated to the backburner. The result is that our souls experience the deep loneliness that God alone can fill. No person, no thing, no achievement, no fame, no wealth can fill the great void in our souls. Only God can. If we see in our souls this great need for love and companionship, today, let us run to the only one who can fill that need.

Prayer:

Lord, please come into my life and fill my heart with your love and your presence. You alone can satisfy me. You alone can fill my need for companionship. You alone can heal my loneliness. I want to be intimately in love with you. Amen.

Wednesday of Week Three

"[Wisdom] is a breath of the power of God, and a pure emanation of the glory of the Almighty; therefore nothing defiled gains entrance into her. For she is a reflection of eternal light, a spotless mirror of the working of God, and an image of his goodness. For [wisdom] is more beautiful than the sun, and excels every constellation of the stars. Compared with the light she is found to be superior, for it is succeeded by the night, but against wisdom evil does not prevail.

- *Cf. Wisdom 7:25 - cf. Wisdom 8:2*

Meditation:

When you and I choose to live in the goodness of God, the natural result of that good life is a spiritual joy and the beauty of a moral life lived well. A life that is filled with truth is one that is peaceful and beautiful. If we live this way, our hearts will be entirely at peace because we know that despite whatever happens exteriorly, our interior state is one with the very source of love itself: God. This is one of the great blessings and splendors of the spiritual life. This is why, one who lives a life full of truth and goodness is often called wise. Because their entire life is ordered rightly in the eyes of both God and man.

Prayer:

Lord, I want to be truly wise, and in order to do that, I must live a life that is full of your truth and goodness. Please fill me with your life that such a life may be my own. Amen.

Thursday of Week Three

"Martyrdom is the supreme witness given to the truth of the faith: it means bearing witness even unto death. The martyr bears witness to Christ who died and rose, to whom he is united by charity. He bears witness to the truth of the faith and of Christian doctrine. He endures death through an act of fortitude. "Let me become the food of the beasts, through whom it will be given me to reach God."

- CCC 2473

Meditation:

Many of us don't often think of being martyrs. Yet, I would like to put to you that, from the day of our baptism, we have all been called to be martyrs for the faith. The word "martyr" from the Greek, "*marturia*" actually means witness. Yet the idea of being a witness and dying for the truth you witness have never been separate in the mind of the Church. From our baptism, we are all called to begin dying to ourselves. Every day, as we lay down our attachments to sin, wealth, power, pleasure, and honor, we are dying to ourselves. In their place, we are called to place our love of God first. From there, we are called to love our fellow man. If we order our lives this way, we will find that we are truly free, truly peaceful, and truly happy. This isn't a quick fix, but it is a worthwhile lifelong process.

Prayer:

Lord, grant me the grace to make those daily steps to die to myself and lay down my attachments to sins, things, and people. Help me love You and others as you want me to. Set me free to be peaceful and happy. Amen.

Friday of Week Three

"The sixth beatitude proclaims, 'Blessed are the pure in heart, for they shall see God.' 'Pure in heart' refers to those who have attuned their intellects and wills to the demands of God's holiness, chiefly in three areas: charity; chastity or sexual rectitude; love of truth and orthodoxy of faith. There is a connection between purity of heart, of body, and of faith."

- CCC 2518

Meditation:

We are all called to be pure of heart. This means that, in the deepest parts of our souls, we have let go of attachment to those things that would corrupt our souls. The Christian life isn't just about saying "no" to things. It is actually about saying a greater "YES!" to more blessed things. When we are careful about what we watch, what we read, what we listen to, what we say, what we do, and who we are close to, we find that we are also free to start watching, listening, reading, saying, and doing good, life-building things. We will find a desire to befriend those who will upbuild us in this blessed life. This is the way all the saints before us have lived their lives. Daily, we slowly but sure choose true, good, and beautiful things, and it builds up into a wellspring within our souls.

Prayer:

Lord, build within me a life filled with all that is blessed and holy. Help me in this walk to become a blessed and holier person. You have called me to sainthood, grant me the grace to live that sainthood here and now. Amen.

Saturday of Week Three

"Keep close to the Catholic Church at all times, for the Church alone can give you true peace, since she alone possesses Jesus, the true Prince of Peace, in the Blessed Sacrament"

- St. Padre Pio

Meditation:

Showing mercy is a very misunderstood act among many Christians. We often think of mercy as wiping out the entirety of the wrong that has been done. In some sense, that is true, but the Church teaches us that there are two consequences to mortal sin, the eternal and the temporal. The eternal consequence of sin is that we have cut off our relationship from God. The Sacrament of Reconciliation restores that bond. However, the temporal consequence of sin is the damage that the sinful act has caused. This is the part we don't often think about. Our sins have consequences that affect ourselves, our brothers and sisters, and the Church. Penance is how we restore the good that has been lost in the relationship. When we ask for mercy, we still have an obligation to work to rebuild the goodwill that has been lost in the relationship. That is the great work of penance that the Church encourages us to during the Season of Lent.

Prayer:

Lord, grant me the courage to accept that my sinful acts have hurt my friends and family members. As I seek forgiveness, and as I forgive others, help me rebuild the goodness lost in these relationships. Amen.

Fourth Sunday of Lent

"For God so loved the world that he gave his only Son, so that everyone who believes in him might not perish but might have eternal life."

- *John 3:16*

Meditation:

Today is Laetare Sunday. It is the Refreshment Sunday of the Lenten Season. Today, the Church calls us to find relief amidst the penitential days of the Lenten season. The Church calls us to celebrate, to taste of sweetness, and joy, and laughter, and enjoy life. Today, the Church reminds us that the work of penance, prayer, fasting, and almsgiving, is meant to culminate in a deeper savoring of the joy of the Gospel of Jesus Christ. This Sunday, the Church is reminding us that we have to keep looking forward to the great Feast of Easter and the Easter Season. Today, the Church reminds us, *we are almost there!* Today, I encourage you and your families to breathe, to relax a little together, to do acts of true, enjoyed leisure, to have a celebratory meal, to have some time to enjoy each other's presence. Today, the Church reminds us: Joy is at the heart of the Gospel.

Prayer:

Lord, grant my family and me a deep taste of the joy you promise to all who profess faith in you. We love you and so we ask you to fill us with joy and love this day and every day of our lives. Amen.

Monday of Week Four

"Rejoice, Jerusalem, and all who love her. Be joyful, all who were in mourning; exalt and be satisfied at her consoling breast."

- Isaiah 66:10-11

Meditation:

A common misrepresentation of Christianity is that it is nothing but a religion of rules. There is a lot that is wrong about that perspective. Christianity is a religion, inasmuch as religion as a virtue means to give to God that which He is owed, i.e. our life in obedience and worship. The rules, therefore, are a reflection of how His children are called to live in His family. The commandments of God are best understood when we see them as the family rules a Father calls His children to live by, not because He is trying to limit their joy, but precisely because He knows that His commandments are the only way we can enjoy a full and flourishing life. When we despair about all that we behold in the world, we also should simultaneously exalt in our Lord because we can always depend on His infinite Fatherly love for us, His covenant children.

Prayer:

Lord, grant me the grace to rejoice in being a child of your family. Enlighten my mind to understand that your commands flow from your deep, Fatherly love for me. Amen.

Tuesday of Week Four

"God, who is the ultimate judge of history, will also know how to understand and accept, in accordance with his justice, the cry of victims, over and above the tones of bitterness that sometimes colours them."

- Benedict XVI, Wednesday Address, 2005

Meditation:

Our human nature hungers for justice. Whether personal, societal, institutional, national, or global; Whenever we behold any injustice, our nature cries out from within us for the resolution of that injustice. We cannot stand to see the undue suffering of our fellow man, especially of those who are innocent. Unfortunately, because of our fallen nature, there are many things that happen in life that prevent us from receiving the justice we are owed. Truth that will not be confessed, apologies that will never be made, and just punishment that will never be meted out. In the face of this, God, our Father, reminds us to cling ever more to Him. He is the ultimate judge and justice is ultimately His. Whatever justice we do not see in this life, we will see in the life to come. That is one of the great assurances of our faith in Christ.

Prayer:

Lord, take my desire for justice. Take my anger and unforgiveness and resentment. Grant me the grace to let go and trust that You will be the Lord who judges all the living and the dead in the life to come. Amen.

Wednesday of Week Four

"Christ has gained for us not only new dignity in our life on earth, but above all the new dignity of the children of God, called to share eternal life with him. Lent invites us to overcome the temptation of seeing the realities of this world as definitive and to recognize that 'our homeland is in heaven' (Phil 3:20)"

- Pope St. John Paul II

Meditation:

Sin warps our intellects. It perverts our view of ourselves and others. In that light, it is very hard to see ourselves as children of God who possess the dignity of being His children. The Lenten season is a good time for us to find rest in the forgiveness of our Father in the Sacrament of Reconciliation, and, from there, to also recognize our dignity restored because of Jesus Christ's finished work on the Cross. The more we cling to Jesus's Cross, the more we are able to let go of the lies of the world. Our identity and our worth is determined by the sum total of God's love for us: infinite.

Prayer:

Lord, change how I see myself. Help me see myself as you do. Help me rest in the dignity of being your child. Help me live a life restored in your forgiveness. Grant me the grace to make a devout confession so that I can be fully united to you and that I can rest in your love. Amen.

Thursday of Week Four

"Lent is a time of truth. Christians, called by the Church to prayer, penance, fasting and self-sacrifice, place themselves before God and recognize themselves; they rediscover themselves."

- Pope St. John Paul II

Meditation:

It is easy to accept lies about ourselves, about others, about God, and about the world, if we don't seek to constantly ground ourselves in the truth of God, who alone is the source and summit of all truth. The Church grants us the grace of the Lenten season so that we can come to face the lies that we have embraced. Lent is a time when we can take a deep and true look at our souls. It is painful and yet necessary for us to let go of these lies so that we can embrace God's love and light. The light of God illuminates all the dark places within our hearts and minds so that we can grow in deeper truth and, therefore, in deeper unity with God. This is why Jesus told us that, "you will come to know the truth, and the truth will set you free" (John 8:31-32).

Prayer:

Lord, fill my soul with an abundance of your light so that all the darkened places of my soul will be illuminated. Remove the lies and the darkness that I have allowed to dwell in my soul. Fill my soul with your life and your truth. Set me free with the truth of your Son, my savior, Jesus Christ. Amen.

Friday of Week Four

"Lent is the favorable time to offer to the Lord sincere thanks for the wonders he has done for humanity in every age, and especially in the Redemption when he did not spare his own Son (cf. Rom 8:32)."

- Pope St. John Paul II

Meditation:

We live in a thankless age. When was the last time you and I dedicated some time to simply pray in thanksgiving to God for all that He has done for us? Lent is a season that encourages us to give our Lord true thanks from the depths of our heart for all that He has done in sending His only begotten Son to suffer and die for us. The Trinity has made themselves a true gift to us in the grace of the Father, the salvation of the Son, and the love of the Holy Spirit. They have been working for the salvation of our souls and they have gifted us so much in our faith and the sacraments. They also continue to bless us with gift upon gift: our work, our families, our health, our life, our wellbeing, our children, and the list goes on. Today, let us take 5 minutes to offer sincere gratitude for everything that the Lord has lavished upon us, His beloved children.

Prayer:

Lord, compel my soul to an overflowing spirit of thankfulness for all that you have done for me. I want to have true gratitude for all that you are in my life. Amen.

Saturday of Week Four

"O Lord and Master of my life, take from me the spirit of sloth, faintheartedness, lust of power, and idle talk. But give rather the spirit of chastity, humility, patience and love to your servant. Yea, O Lord and King, grant me to see my own sin and not to judge my brother, for You are blessed from all ages to all ages. Amen"

- St. Ephraim the Syrian

Meditation:

Our Lenten journey is filled with prayer, fasting, almsgiving, and penance. All of these are good practices that grant us the avenue to die to our selfish desires and to foster greater selflessness within us. This selflessness should overflow from within us for the good of others as well. The more we do these things in the right spirit and the grace of God, the more we are conformed to the heart of God. God wants to set us free from all the chains that bind us in the slavery of sin, no matter how small. He knows that when we are set free, we are more disposed to love Him and others. Today, let us pray for the grace of ongoing freedom from all sin and inordinate attachments so that we can be truly disposed to love God and our fellow brothers and sisters.

Prayer:

Lord, set me free more and more each day, that I might be able to let go of my own self-centeredness and that I might be more deliberate in loving you and my brothers and sisters. Amen.

Fifth Sunday of Lent

"Jesus is revealed as the word of the new and everlasting covenant: divine freedom and human freedom have definitively met in his crucified flesh, in an indissoluble and eternally valid compact. Jesus himself, at the Last Supper, in instituting the Eucharist, had spoken of a "new and everlasting covenant" in the outpouring of his blood, and shows himself to be the true sacrificial Lamb who brings about our definitive liberation from slavery."

- Pope Benedict XVI, Verbum Domini 12

Meditation:

Sometimes when we attend the Holy Mass, it can be tempting to listen to Father's homily and feel like we were "not fed" by it. I want to caution us against this kind of thought or attitude. It has no place in our Catholic life. Every homily, no matter how bad we think it is, is able to teach us at least ONE thing we can take away in our daily growth in holiness. The other, greater reality of the Holy Mass is that the homily is not meant to "feed" us. It is meant to break open the Word of God to us, from which we have already been fed, and to prepare our hearts for the table of the Eucharist, the Word made Flesh, from which we are going to be fed. In short, every time we are at Mass, we are always being fed from the finest food of all: Word and Sacrament.

Prayer:

Lord, help me see just how richly I am being fed at every Holy Mass I attend. Amen.

Monday of Week Five

"The first commandments are not cruel, nor are the second hard and grievous, but all come from one and the same providential care. Hear the affirmation of the prophet that God gave the old covenant also, or rather (so we must speak), the affirmation of him who is both the one and the other."

- St. John Chrysostom

Meditation:

The Old and New Testaments are not disconnected. They speak to us of the one Father who, throughout human history, has been pursuing man so that He can espouse them to Himself. God is an eternally loving Father. He is truly Father in a way that human fathers will never be able to live up to. His love is the only love that is fully true. So, when we see the events in the Old Testament that speak to God's divine justice, we are seeing the loving hand of a Father who knows that His children need to be disciplined and guided into the only life that they will flourish in and find full happiness. Jesus's life on earth modeled for us the truest standard of how we ought to live as children of the Father. Because the Father infinitely loves us, He gives us His grace to enable us to not only live as Christ lived, but also to unite us to the heart of the Father, Son, and Holy Spirit. This is love like no other. And this love is now ours.

Prayer:

Lord, show me how much you love me. Help me know it, feel it, be filled with it, and live it. Amen.

Tuesday of Week Five

"Behold, Jesus Christ crucified, who is the only foundation of our hope; He is our mediator and advocate; the victim and sacrifice for our sins. He is goodness and patience itself; His mercy is moved by the tears of sinners, and he never refuses pardon and grace to those who ask it with a truly contrite and humbled heart."

- St. Charles Borromeo

Meditation:

The Crucifixion of Christ is the single worst moral act of mankind in human history. We killed the God who loves us so infinitely that He became like us. And yet, we must not forget that this was a sacrifice that Jesus willingly offered Himself for. This terrible historical event became, by God's power and grace, the greatest event of man's salvation. This was the moment that won for us so great a reunification to God the Father. Christ reversed not only the ugliness of the Crucifixion but also the effect of sin and death itself. Now, death has no power over us. Sin has no power over us. Provided we run to and cling to Christ's grace constantly, we are free from the sting and pain of sin, death, and hell. God took the greatest injustice in human history and transformed it to the greatest salvific act of God in human history. How great is the love of our God.

Prayer:

Lord, unite me to your Cross. Unite me to the love that drew you to the Cross. And unite me to the salvation that flows forth from your death on the Cross. Amen.

Wednesday of Week Five

"As Lent is the time for greater love, listen to Jesus' thirst...He knows your weakness. He wants only your love, wants only the chance to love you."

- St. Teresa of Calcutta

Meditation:

Mother Teresa was deeply attuned to the dark night of her soul. For decades, she endured so much interior desolation. She didn't enjoy euphoric emotional highs that so many of us hunger for in spiritual experiences. Yet, Mother Teresa emulated true Christian faithfulness by staying true to the call that God had placed in her life. One of the pitfalls we can run into in the Christian life is to believe that God only speaks to us through consolation. Recognizing the love of God the Father means knowing that He is infinitely loving to us through all seasons of our life, consolation, peace, or desolation. God calls us to the faithfulness of being His children and, as is the case in all family life, not all experiences will be consoling or euphoric. Yet, all family life is meant to make us grow in holiness.

Prayer:

Lord, help me continue to seek you and to fall deeper in love with you through all seasons of life, especially when I am experiencing desolation. As much as my soul thirsts for you, you say that you thirst for me as well. Help me respond to that with total surrender to you. Amen.

Thursday of Week Five

"Fasting cleanses the soul, raises the mind, subjects one's flesh to the spirit, renders the heart contrite and humble, scatters the clouds of concupiscence, quenches the fire of lust, and kindles the true light of chastity. Enter again into yourself."

- St. Augustine of Hippo

Meditation:

We gravitate away from the uncomfortable. No one likes being put in a situation where we feel discomfort. Yet, the Lenten season is about embracing those good things that often make our fallen human nature uncomfortable, so that we can be freer to be united to God. This is why we fast, and pray, and give alms, and do penance. We want to have our sinfulness, and our concupiscence, and our pride dispelled from within us. These Lenten practices allow for us to lay down ourselves in small ways daily so that we can embrace greater ways of laying down ourselves for the sake of God and others. These practices are meant to build within us deeper lives of virtue. This is why we ought to ensure that our Lenten experience is one saturated in happy prayer and reading Scripture. The more we are joined to the source of life, the more life we will feel within us.

Prayer:

Lord, help me enjoy the works of prayer, fasting, penance, and almsgiving. I want to be greater joined to your love this season of Lent. Amen.

Friday of Week Five

"Let us set out with trust on our Lenten journey, sustained by fervent prayer, penance and concern for those in need. In particular, may this Lent be a time of ever greater concern for the needs of children, in our own families and in society as a whole: for they are the future of humanity."

- Pope St. John Paul II

Meditation:

It is a true injustice that so many think that we ought to be kinder to people outside of our family instead of the other way around. We ought to strive to reserve our best selves for our spouses, our children, our siblings, or our parents. Parents need to begin modeling this. Being family doesn't give us the right of unkindness to our family members. If anything, we are called to greater charity and kindness to the members of our family, compared to anyone else. If we live ordering our lives rightly, loving God, our spouse, our children, our siblings or parents, and then our work and others in our life, we will find that this right ordering transforms us into the best version of ourselves: virtuous children of God the Father.

Prayer:

Lord, change me to be truly loving toward my family, especially if I have developed a mentality of taking them for granted. Change me to love them as you want me to love them. Amen.

Saturday of Week Five

"The purpose of Lent is not to force on us a few formal obligations, but to 'soften' our heart so that it may open itself to the realities of the spirit, to experience the hidden 'thirst' for communion with God."

- Pope St. John Paul II

Meditation:

Prayers, fasting, almsgiving, and penance are difficult things to do. They are painful. They are sacrificial. They are not easy. And yet, the Church reminds us that when we engage in these works in Lent, our hearts are not hardened. Instead, these works break away the hardened parts of our hearts. Conversely, indulgence in sin, in wealth, pleasure, power, and honor, these are the things that harden our hearts. When we undertake Christian sacrifice, we find that God cooperates with us. He removes from us the hardened heart that we might have developed. He grants us hearts of love. We will find that loving ourselves, loving others and, ultimately, loving God, become easier things to do. In fact, we will find ourselves hungering for and thirsting for the love of God more and more.

Prayer:

Lord, make me hunger and thirst for you. Take my heart of stone and give me a heart like yours, truly loving and selfless. Make love easy for me. Let love flow from within me constantly because I am united to you. Amen.

Palm Sunday

"Holy Week, which for Christians is the most important week of the year, gives us the opportunity to immerse ourselves in the central events of the Redemption, to relive the Paschal Mystery, the great Mystery of faith."

- Pope Benedict XVI, Holy Week, 2009

Meditation:

We have made it to the climax of Lent. In truth, Passion Week is the climax of the Christian life. The Church deliberately structures the Lenten season in this way so that we can be so fully immersed in the events of Holy Week or Passion Week. Today, we enter into Palm Sunday alongside Jesus Christ. We join the crowd crying out, "Hosanna to the Son of David! Blessed is He who comes in the Name of the Lord, Hosanna in the Highest!" (Matthew 21:9). The throng recognizes in the person of Jesus a marked difference in the history of Israel. Yet, even as He enters Jerusalem, Jesus has one thing in mind: His impending Paschal mystery. Nothing will deter Him from this final mission. Christ's submissive obedience to this salvific plan of the Father is a sobering call for us this Lent.

Prayer:

Lord, today, I, with the crowd, celebrate your kingship. Yet, your Crucifixion looms ahead. Ready my soul to join you in your journey to the Upper Room and to Calvary, so that I can genuinely savor your Resurrection to come. Amen.

Monday of Holy Week

"The tragedy of the passion brings to fulfillment our own life and the whole of human history. We can't let Holy Week be just a kind of commemoration. It means contemplating the mystery of Jesus Christ as something which continues to work in our souls."

- Saint Josemaria Escriva

Meditation:

Every year, we enter into Holy Week and, for many of us, the emotional toll is felt. The Liturgies of Holy Week are longer, the readings are more intense, and the prayers and liturgical actions are more somber. This is by design. Holy Mother Church intentionally does this so that her children can immerse themselves in intellect, will, and passion in the suffering of their Lord. Our Lord Jesus went into Jerusalem in order to embrace the Cross. He didn't shy away from it, He didn't seek to escape it. He sought to do the will of the Father, no matter how painful that will might be for Him. He knew that His salvific work was going to be a ransom for all mankind and this was why He was sent into the world. Let us enter into Jesus's heart this week. He embraced mortal death for us so that we could embrace everlasting life with Him.

Prayer:

Lord, this week, open my soul to be immersed fully in the experience of your Passion. Let me be so united to you that I will experience all the fruits of your saving work. Amen.

Tuesday of Holy Week

"O souls! Seek a refuge, like pure doves, in the shadow of the crucifix. There, mourn the Passion of your divine Spouse, and drawing from your hearts flames of love and rivers of tears, make of them a precious balm with which to anoint the wounds of your Savior."

- St. Paul of the Cross

Meditation:

The Cross is undesirable. It is painful, it is miserable, and it brings death. The crosses we experience in our daily human life are no different, albeit on a smaller scale. And yet, Jesus modeled for us the true path of Christianity: to run to and cling to the Cross. What was once an historical instrument of tortuous execution is now an everlasting sign of man's salvation. What was once the instrument of earthly power of a temporary empire is now the everlasting sign of divine power in triumphing over sin and death. The shadow of the cross is not darkness, it is the light of Christian life. In the shadow of Christ's cross, we see our true selves. We see the effects of sin on our soul, and we see the immense power of God to deliver us from our own sinfulness and to cleanse and heal and draw us into His own divine life.

Prayer:

Lord, grant me the grace to cling to you upon the Cross. Help me hold the Cross close to me, as the sign of my own deliverance. In that light, give meaning to the daily crosses of my life. Amen.

Wednesday of Holy Week

"We give glory to you, Lord, who raised up your cross to span the jaws of death like a bridge by which souls might pass from the region of the dead to the land of the living. ..You are incontestably alive. Your murderers sowed your living body in the earth as farmers sow grain, but it sprang up and yielded an abundant harvest of men raised from the dead."

- Saint Ephrem the Syrian

Meditation:

This week, Jesus does some of the most unthinkable things leading up to His Crucifixion. He enters Jerusalem riding upon a donkey and is greeted as a true King and Son of David would be; He cleanses the Temple in Jerusalem of the money changers and traders; and He predicts the destruction of the Temple and Jerusalem (which wouldn't take place until 70 A.D.). In all these events, one cannot help but see the impending death that He was to undergo. All of these events were precursors to His death. It is hard for us to imagine, but being fully God, He spent every day of that week waking up realizing the kind of death He was to undergo for the salvation of all. And it undoubtedly weighed upon His human soul. So what did He do? He prayed to His Father.

Prayer:

Lord, in times when I am in most anguish, help me run to you in prayer even more. Amen.

Holy Thursday

"Jesus called God 'Abba.' The word means – as they add – 'Father.' Yet it is not the usual form of the word 'father,' but rather a children's word – an affectionate name which one would not have dared to use in speaking to God. It is the language of the one who is truly a 'child,' the Son of the Father, the one who is conscious of being in communion with God, in deepest union with him."

- Pope Benedict XVI, Holy Thursday, 2012

Meditation:

On Holy Thursday, Our Lord Jesus Christ establishes the New and Eternal Covenant in His blood, he ordains the Apostles as bishops of His Church, and He goes to the Mount of Olives to pray. There, He cries out to His Father, as a child would. He pours His heart out in prayer to His Father with the kind of trust that only a trusting child of a truly good Father could. Jesus knows the goodness of the Father. He knows that in the Father alone is His deepest and truest consolation. Our fallen human nature constantly seeks consolation in other things or people. Yet, only God suffices. Only God satisfies. Today, let us join Jesus in seeking consolation from the heart of the Father.

Prayer:

Lord, today I join Jesus in the Garden of Gethsemane. I offer you all my anguish and concern. I want to trust in your goodness toward me. Be the great source of my consolation. Amen.

Good Friday

"Christianity, unlike any other religion in the world, begins with catastrophe and defeat. Sunshine religions and psychological inspirations collapse in calamity and wither in adversity. But the Life of the Founder of Christianity, having begun with the Cross, ends with the empty tomb and victory."

- Archbishop Fulton Sheen, *Life of Christ*

Meditation:

Today, we walk with Jesus on the Way of the Cross. This is the most painful day in the Liturgical calendar. We stand beside Jesus as He is scourged, watching Him bleed; we watch Him carry His Cross amidst His immense pain, we watch Him hold the heartbreak of betrayal and abandonment within His soul, and we watch Him get Crucified and die. The pain and anguish of this day cannot be understated. But we need to bear in mind that Jesus did this for us. This is why we are Christian. This is why we profess faith in Christ. He undertook all of this for the sake of paying the debt of sin that separated us from the infinite Love of God the Father. His death is our doorway to eternal life.

Prayer:

Lord, amidst my tears and heartbreak for all that Jesus underwent for me, help me keep in mind your immense love that won for me so great a savior and so great a reunification with you. Amen.

Holy Saturday

"To be Christians means to share personally in the Death and Resurrection of Christ. This sharing is brought about sacramentally by Baptism, upon which, as a solid foundation, the Christian life of each one of us is built."

- Pope St. John Paul II

Meditation:

We witness Jesus get placed in the tomb. We stand outside the tomb as the stone is rolled to cover the entrance. It is easy to imagine why His apostles lost their faith. Death seems to always have the final say. Yet, tonight, something completely unique in human history happened 2000 years ago. Christ conquered death. He raised Himself from the dead. The stone was rolled away without human assistance. Eyewitness testimony proves the historical reality of our faith. Jesus Christ rose from the dead! We get to celebrate with the anticipation of the Church today. The empty tomb and the darkness of the night are signs of our hope and anticipation for the all-powerful light and love of God that has come into the world to dispel the darkness of our life once and for all.

Prayer:

Lord, today, illuminate the darkest parts of my life and my soul. Help me feel the anticipation that Mary and the women felt, knowing that my beloved Jesus has conquered my sin and my death. Amen.

Easter Sunday

"Jesus rises from the grave. Life is stronger than death. Good is stronger than evil. Love is stronger than hate. Truth is stronger than lies. The darkness of the previous days is driven away the moment Jesus rises from the grave and himself becomes God's pure light."

- Pope Benedict XVI, Easter Sunday, 2012

Meditation:

Light has broken amidst the darkest moment of human history. The greatest sin of mankind: killing the Son of God, has become the very instrument of all of humanity's salvation. God has conquered our fallenness! Satan has been defeated! The work of evil has been destroyed. Sin and death have lost the final say. God has triumphed. He has won mankind back to Himself. Today, the choice is laid before us: life or death, light or darkness. God loves us just the way we are but He wants to take us from our present state and elevate us into His own Holiness and divine life. This is unthinkable, if not for the omnipotence of God Himself! Today, let the light of God permeate and transcend your entire family and your Easter celebration. May you and your family have a joyous Easter season ahead.

Prayer:

Lord, let the light and power of your resurrection completely permeate and transform every facet of our family life. Let us be entirely yours. Amen.

Conclusion

Thank you for joining us for this Lenten Mission, and for journeying through this companion booklet. It has been our true joy to journey with you through this transformative Liturgical season.

The Christian call is the call to Sainthood. There are many paths to that journey to Sainthood but, ultimately, the great feast of Christianity assures us that as we keep running to the table of the Word and the Eucharist, we will get more and more conformed into the image of Christ.

Our hope is that, in your journeying with us this Lent, this will be a means of a greater walk to Sainthood in your own life. Living the joy of the Easter season entails shining forth the light of the resurrected Christ that emanates from within us. The reason His light emanates from within us is because we, firstly, have allowed Him to permeate us with His transforming love.

Christ loves us just the way we are, but He loves us far too much to leave us that way. He meets us where we are at and He compels us to rise up, to walk, to run, to soar, and to eternally dwell with Him in Happiness. This is the joy of the Gospel. Where once death meant eternal darkness, now, mortal death becomes the gateway to eternal life in God.

The joy that you have experienced, we sincerely hope you will take forth and share with others. As Luke reminds us in the Book of Acts, ""He commissioned us to preach to the people and testify that he is the one appointed by God as judge of the living and the dead. To him all the prophets bear witness, that everyone who believes in him will receive forgiveness of sins through his name" (Acts 10:42-43).

May the joy of Christ burst forth from within you the way the light of Christ burst forth from the tomb wherein He laid. Let this Easter season transform you and your family and, through all of you, may the world be transformed for the love of Christ. God Bless you all. Have a joyous Easter season.

www.ingramcontent.com/pod-product-compliance
Lightning Source LLC
Chambersburg PA
CBHW060844050426
42453CB00008B/819